Step by Step Christmas Songb

Book One

10 Piano Solos with Optional Accompaniments
by Glenda Austin

Orchestrations by Eric Baumgartner

PLAYBACK+
Speed • Pitch • Balance • Loop

To access audio, visit:
www.halleonard.com/mylibrary

Enter Code
6588-9664-3286-9126

ISBN 978-1-5400-3010-8

WILLIS MUSIC

EXCLUSIVELY DISTRIBUTED BY
HAL•LEONARD®

Visit Hal Leonard Online at
www.halleonard.com

Contact Us:
Hal Leonard
7777 West Bluemound Road
Milwaukee, WI 53213
Email: info@halleonard.com

In Europe contact:
Hal Leonard Europe Limited
Distribution Centre, Newmarket Road
Bury St Edmunds, Suffolk, IP33 3YB
Email: info@halleonardeurope.com

In Australia contact:
Hal Leonard Australia Pty. Ltd.
4 Lentara Court
Cheltenham, Victoria, 3192 Australia
Email: info@halleonard.com.au

I love Christmas. These seasonal arrangements were written with a beginning piano student in mind – that's you! The collection includes three new and simple Christmas songs that I hope you will enjoy singing and learning. I have included some questions below for you and your teacher to talk about before learning each piece.

I hope you have a wonderful holiday season.

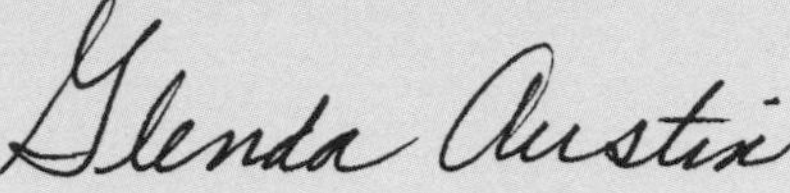
Glenda Austin

Snowing, Snowing!
What measure shares Middle C? (Both hands get to play it!)

Bells Are Ringing
1. Find measures that are ALIKE.
2. Find 2 measures that are ALMOST alike.

One Shining Star
Find 5 notes going DOWN in a row.

Jingle Bells
Find two LINES (or "phrases") that are identical.

Jolly Old St. Nicholas
What are *rests*? What is the ONLY kind of rest in this song?

How Great Our Joy
What are *dynamics*? How many different dynamic marks can you find?

Good King Wenceslas
Which hand plays the last measure?
(I'll give you the answer for this one: either hand! If you have dainty thumbs, BOTH!)

I Saw Three Ships
What count begins the song?
What is a *tie*?

O Come, Little Children
What does it mean to play "with a steady beat"?

O Come, O Come, Emmanuel
What is an *octave*? Can you find the octave in this song?

4 Snowing, Snowing!

5 Bells Are Ringing

6 One Shining Star

8 Jingle Bells

10 Jolly Old St. Nicholas

12 How Great Our Joy

14 Good King Wenceslas

16 I Saw Three Ships

18 O Come, Little Children

20 O Come, O Come, Emmanuel

Snowing, Snowing!

The student is ready to learn this piece after page 19 of *Step by Step,* Book 1.

Words and Music by
Glenda Austin

Joyfully
3 2 1
1
Snow- ing, snow - ing, snow - ing, snow- ing! Such a love - ly day! The

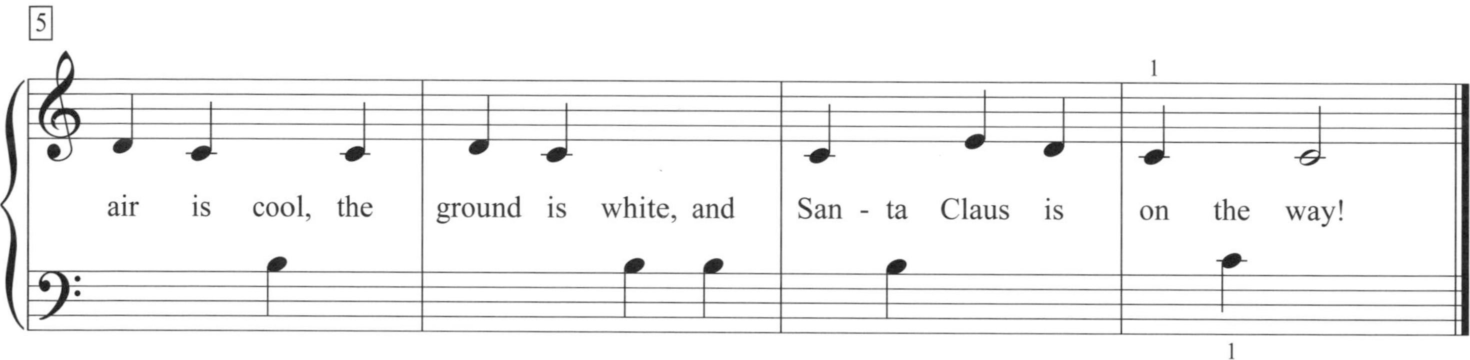
5
1
air is cool, the ground is white, and San - ta Claus is on the way!
1

Accompaniment (Student plays one octave higher than written.)

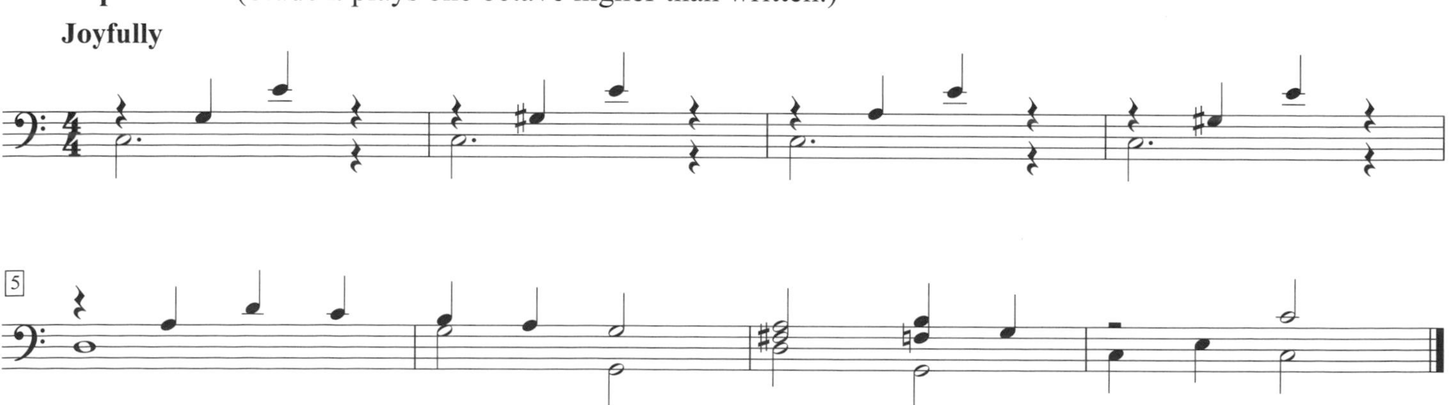
Joyfully
5

Bells Are Ringing

Use after page 21.

Words and Music by
Glenda Austin

With excitement

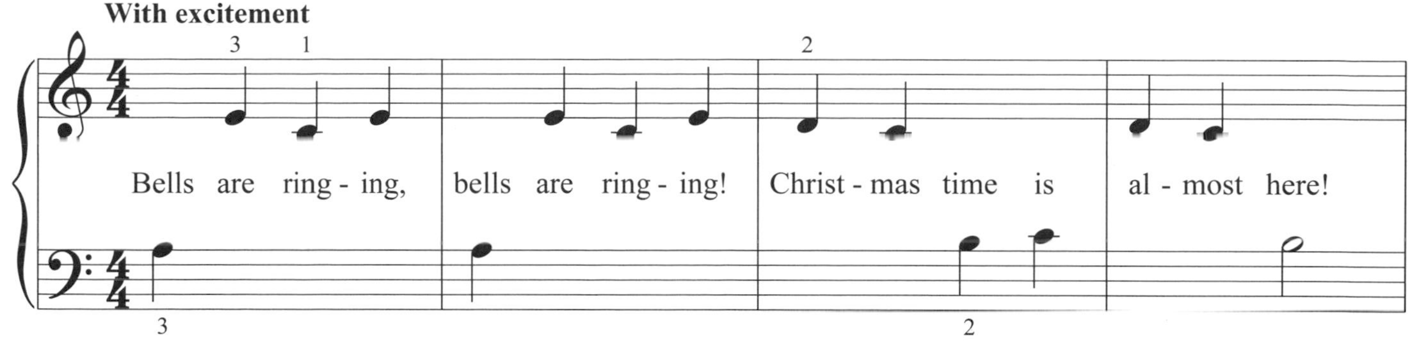
3 1
2
Bells are ring - ing, bells are ring - ing! Christ - mas time is al - most here!
3
2

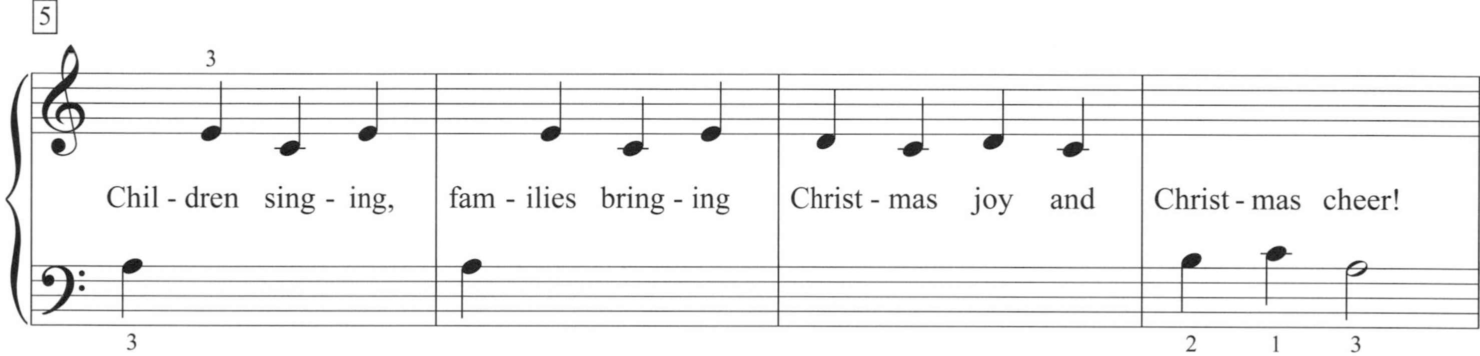
5
3
Chil - dren sing - ing, fam - ilies bring - ing Christ - mas joy and Christ - mas cheer!
3
2 1 3

9
3
Ding
Ding
Dong!
3

Accompaniment (Student plays one octave higher than written.)

With excitement

5
9

© 2018 by The Willis Music Co.
International Copyright Secured All Rights Reserved

One Shining Star

Use after page 24.

Words and Music by
Glenda Austin

With hope, not too slow
3
One shin - ing star on Christ - mas night,
3 1

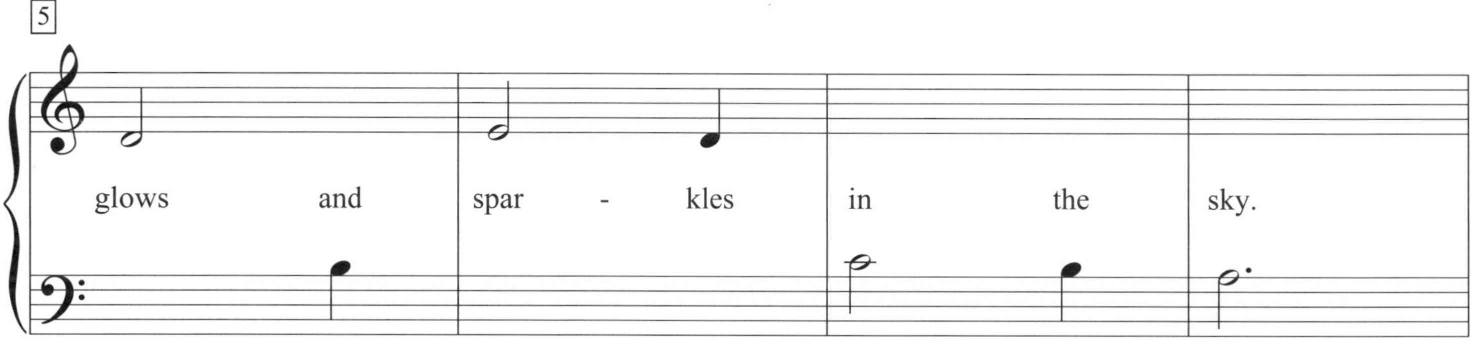
5
glows and spar - kles in the sky.

Accompaniment (Student plays one octave higher than written.)

With hope, not too slow

5

9
3
Bring - ing good - will to all the earth,
3

13
cel - e - brate the Sav - ior's birth.
1

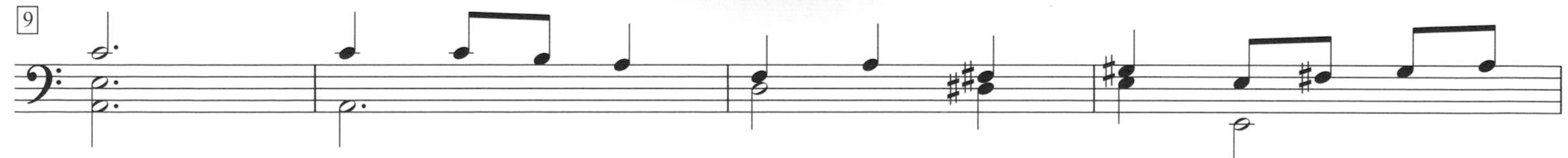
9

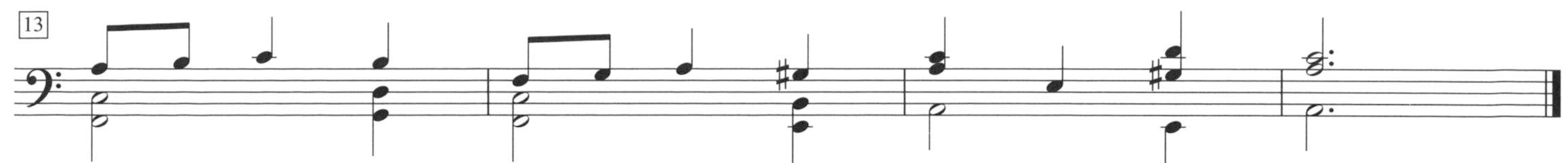
13

Jingle Bells

Use after page 30.

Words and Music by James Lord Pierpont
Arranged by Glenda Austin

Bouncy and lively
2
Jin - gle bells,
jin - gle bells,
jin - gle all the
way.
mf
2
4

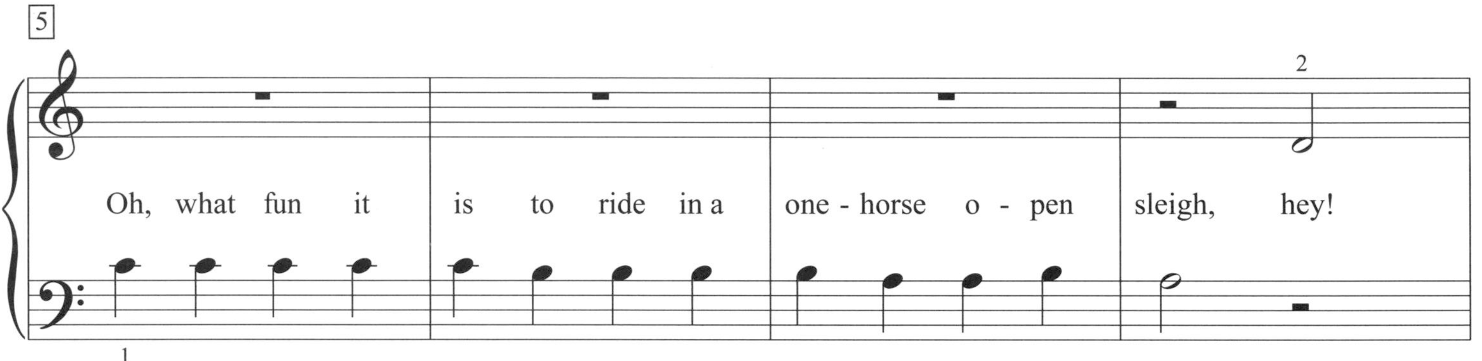
5
2
Oh, what fun it
is to ride in a
one - horse o - pen
sleigh, hey!
1

mf means medium loud.

Accompaniment (Student plays one octave higher than written.)

Bouncy and lively
mf
5

9
Jin - gle bells,
jin - gle bells,
jin - gle all the
way.
2

13
Oh, what fun it
is to ride in a
one - horse o - pen
sleigh!
1

9
13

Jolly Old St. Nicholas

Use after page 34.

19th Century American Carol
Arranged by Glenda Austin

Moderately fast, peppy
3
Jol - ly old Saint
Nich - o - las,
lean your ear this
way!
mf

5
Don't you tell a
sin - gle soul
2
what I'm going to
say.
3
1

Accompaniment (Student plays one octave higher than written.)

Moderately fast, peppy

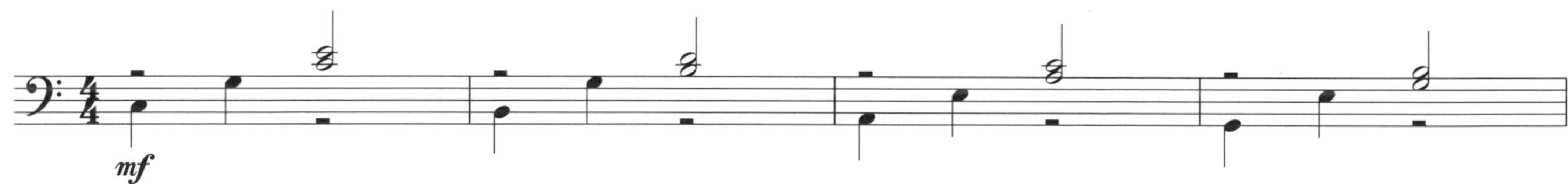
mf

5

9
Christ - mas Eve is com - ing soon, now you dear old man,

13
2
whis - per what you'll bring to me; tell me if you can.
3

9

13

How Great Our Joy

(While by Our Sheep)

Use after page 35.

Traditional German Carol
Arranged by Glenda Austin

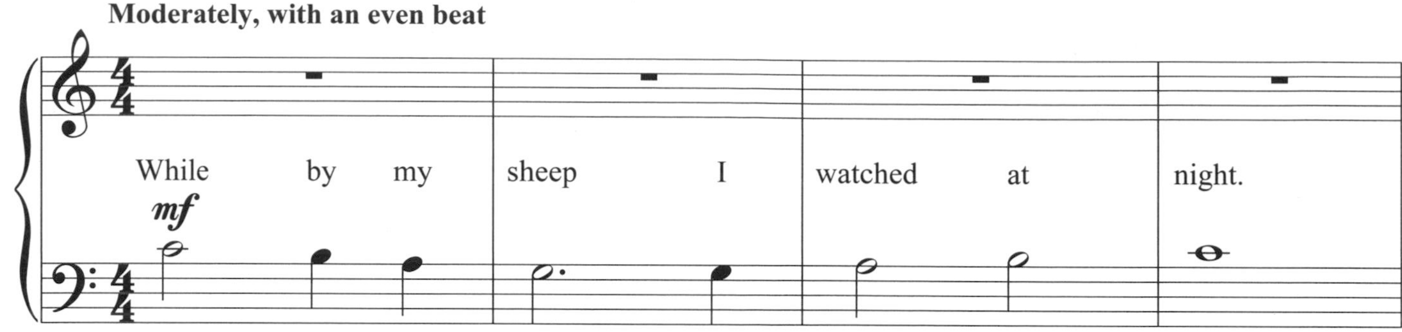
Moderately, with an even beat
While by my sheep I watched at night.
mf

5
Glad tid - ings brought an an - gel bright. How
f

9
great my joy, great my joy.
p

Accompaniment (Student plays one octave higher than written.)

Moderately, with an even beat
mf
5
9
f
p

© 2018 by The Willis Music Co.
International Copyright Secured All Rights Reserved

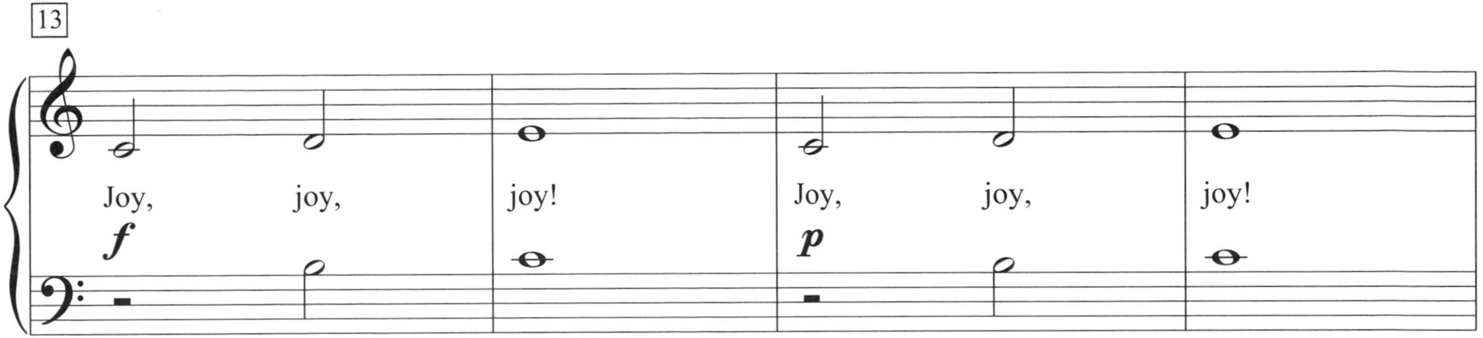
13
Joy, joy, joy! Joy, joy, joy!
f
p

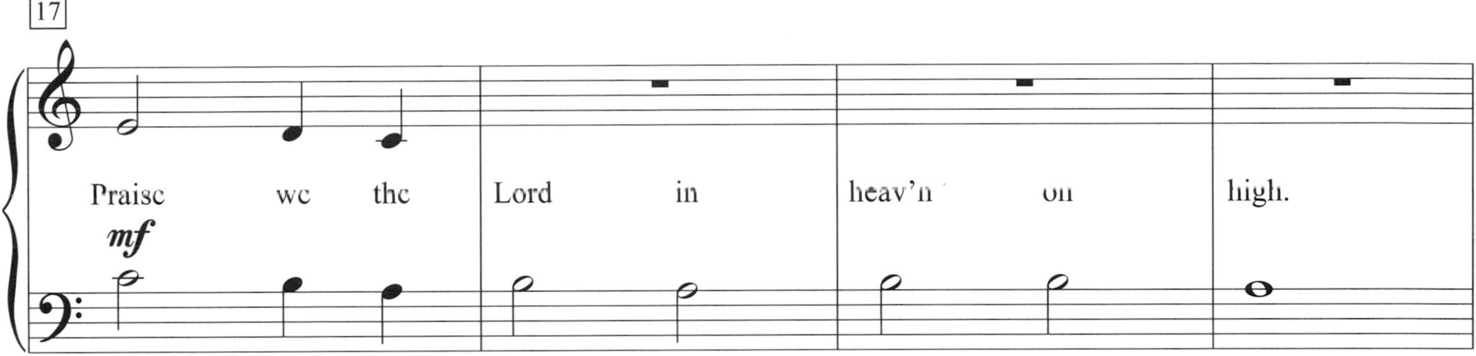
17
Praise we the Lord in heav'n on high.
mf

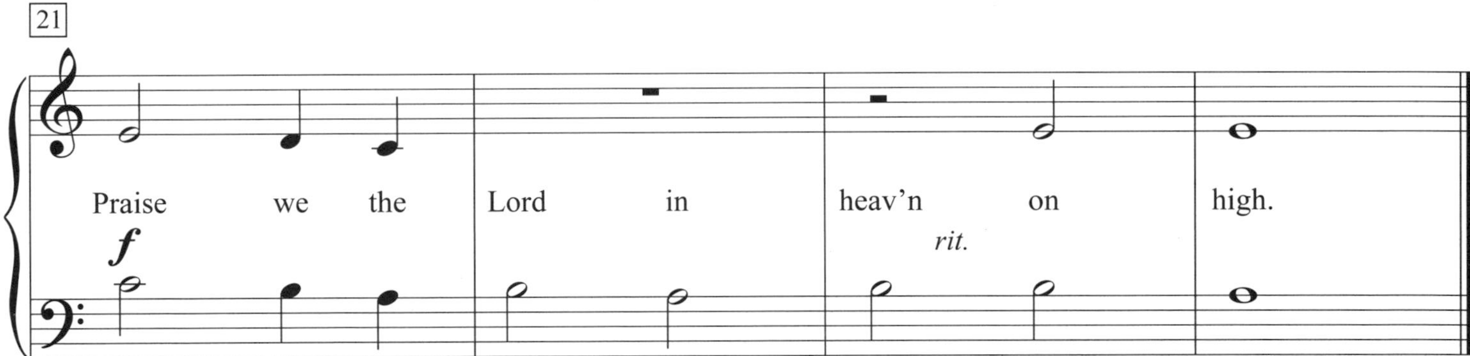
21
Praise we the Lord in heav'n on high.
f
rit.

f means loud. (Play even louder than ***mf***)
p means soft.
rit. means slow down.

13
f
p
17
mf
21
f
rit.

Good King Wenceslas

Use after page 37.

Words by John M. Neale
Music from *Piae Cantiones*
Arranged by Glenda Austin

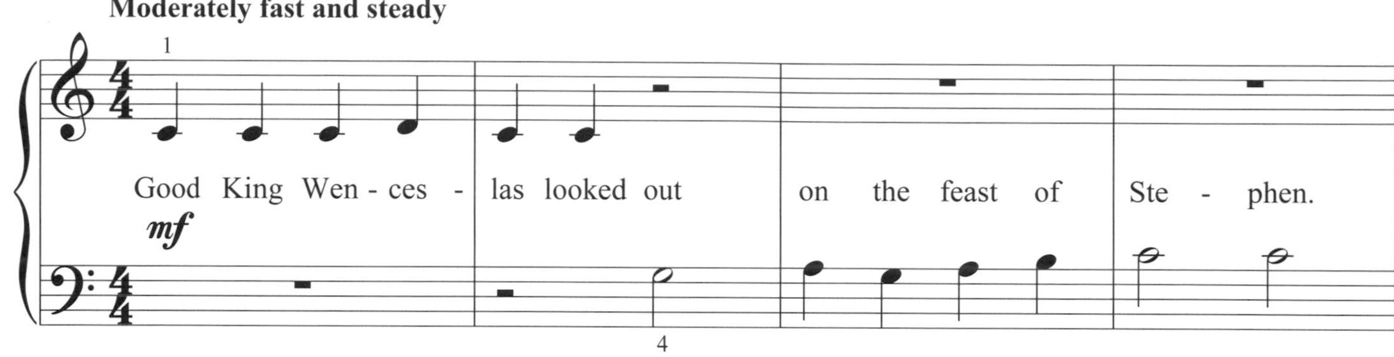
Moderately fast and steady
1
Good King Wen - ces - las looked out on the feast of Ste - phen.
mf
4

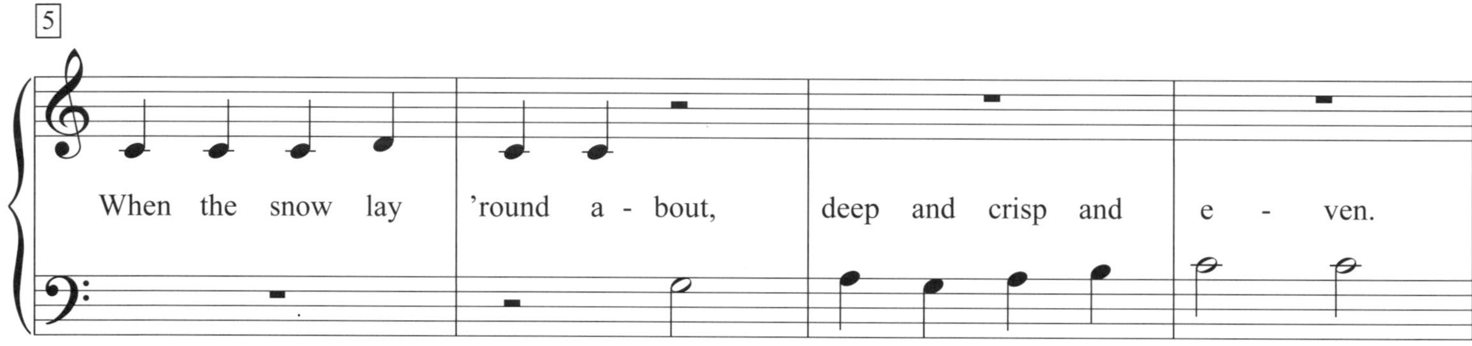
5
When the snow lay 'round a - bout, deep and crisp and e - ven.

Accompaniment (Student plays one octave higher than written.)

Moderately fast and steady
mf
5

© 2018 by The Willis Music Co.
International Copyright Secured All Rights Reserved

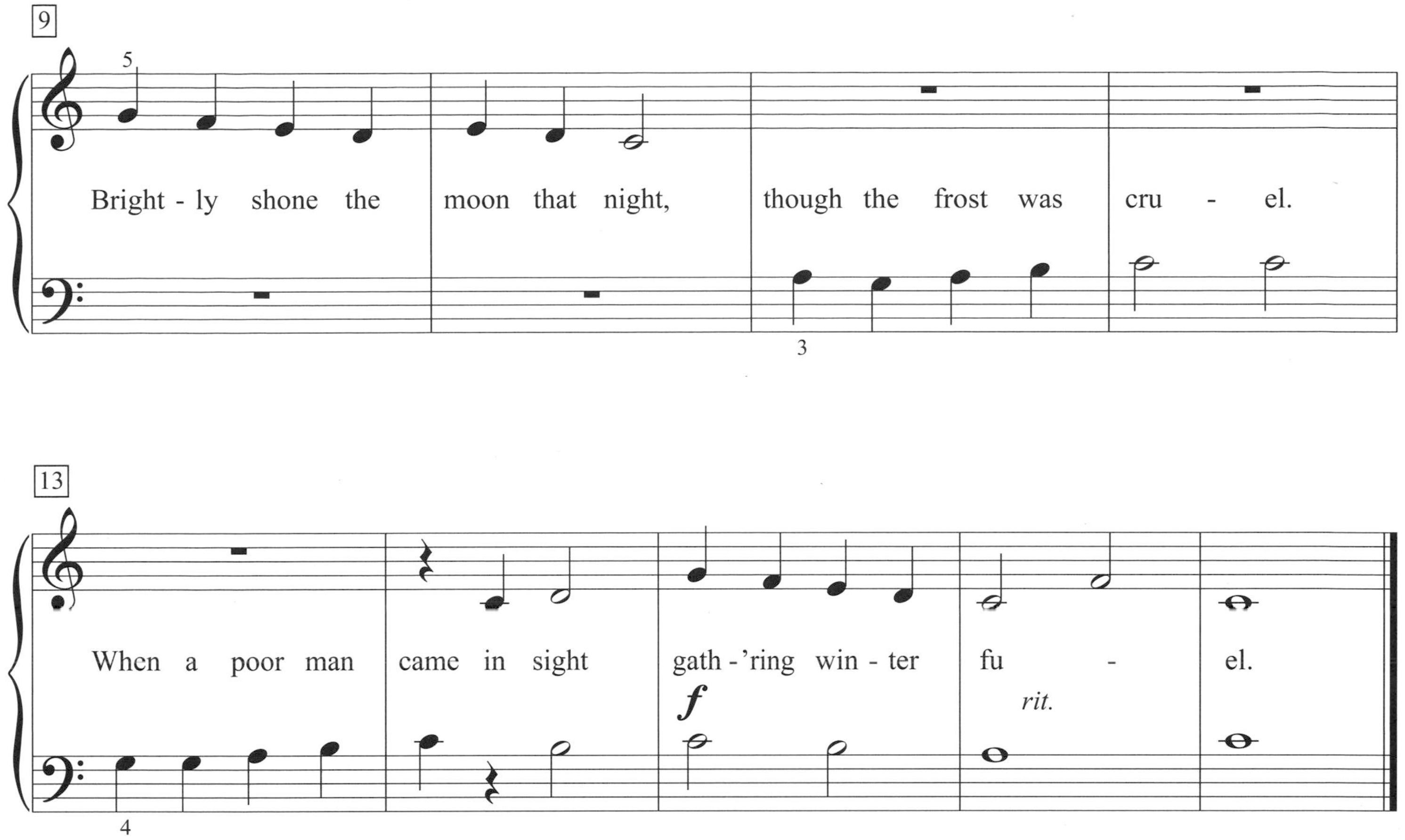

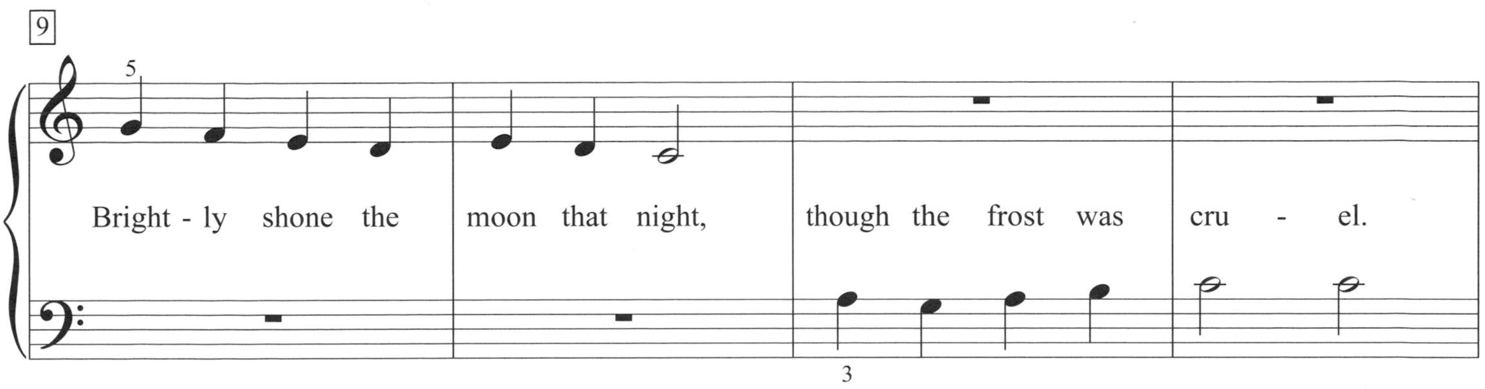
9
5
Bright - ly shone the moon that night, though the frost was cru - el.
3

13

When a poor man came in sight gath - 'ring win - ter fu - el.

f *rit.*

4

9
13
f
rit.

I Saw Three Ships

18th Century English Carol
Arranged by Glenda Austin

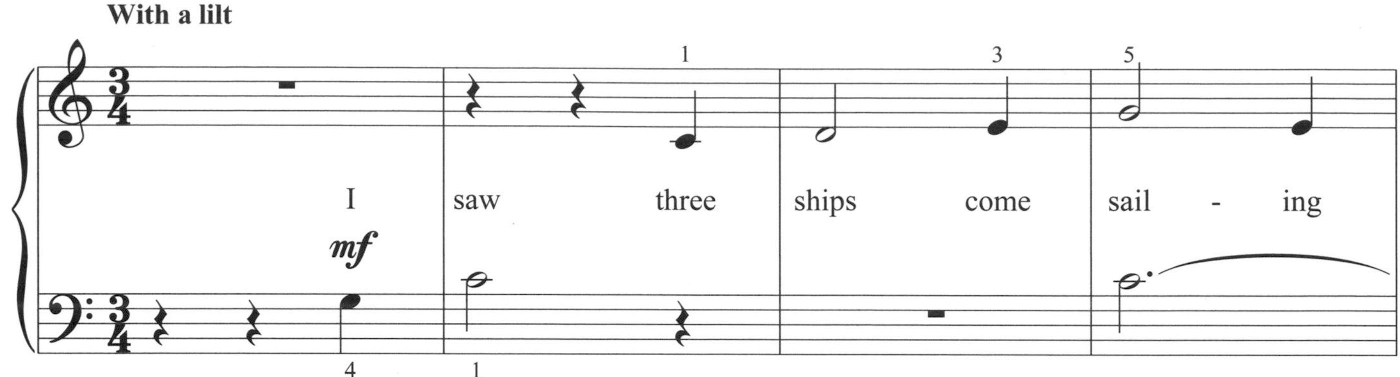
With a lilt
1
3
5
I
saw
three
ships
come
sail
-
ing
mf
4
1

5
in
on
Christ
-
mas
Day,
on
Christ
-
mas
2

Accompaniment (Student plays one octave higher than written.)

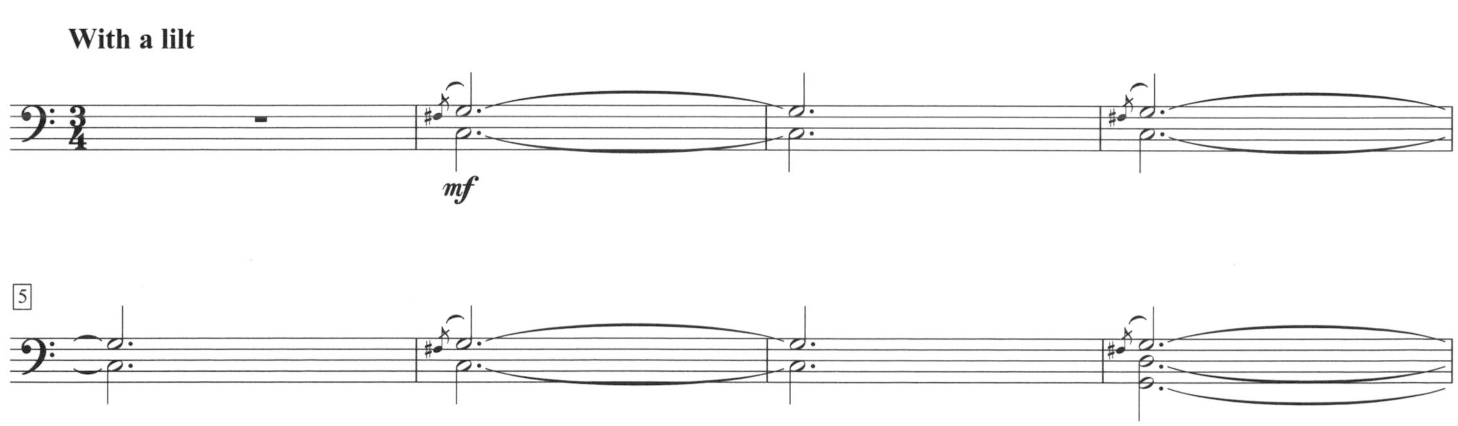
With a lilt
mf
5

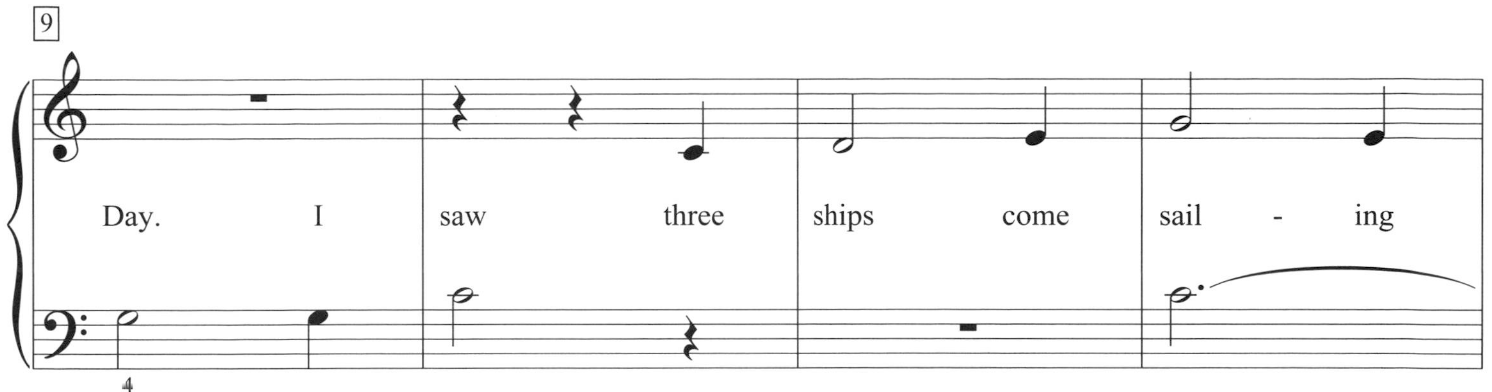
9
Day. I saw three ships come sail - ing
4

13
in on Christ - mas Day in the morn - ing.

9

13

O Come, Little Children

Words by Christoph von Schmidt
Music by Johann A.P. Schulz
Arranged by Glenda Austin

Moderately fast, with a steady beat

2
O come, lit - tle chil - dren, from cot and from
mp
2

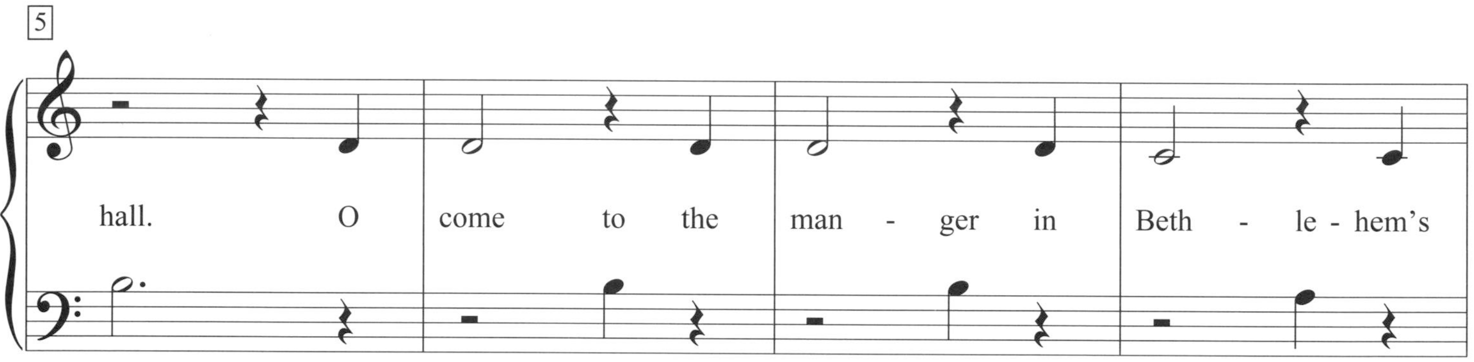
5
hall. O come to the man - ger in Beth - le - hem's

mp means medium soft.

Accompaniment (Student plays one octave higher than written.)

Moderately fast, with a steady beat
mp
5

9
stall. There meek - ly He li - eth, the heav - en - ly Child. So

14
poor and so hum - ble, so sweet and so mild.
rit.

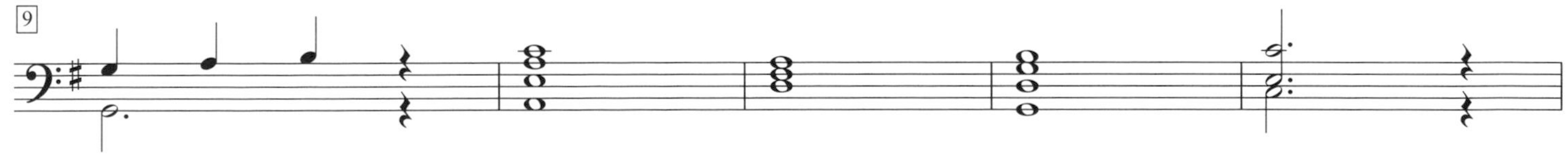
9

14
rit.

O Come, O Come, Emmanuel

Traditional Latin Text
15th Century French Melody
Arranged by Glenda Austin

Moderately, smoothly
1 3
2 4
O
come, O come, Em - man - u - el, and
mp
3

5
ran - som cap - tive Is - ra - el. That mourns in lone - ly
3 1
2

Accompaniment (Student plays one octave higher than written.)

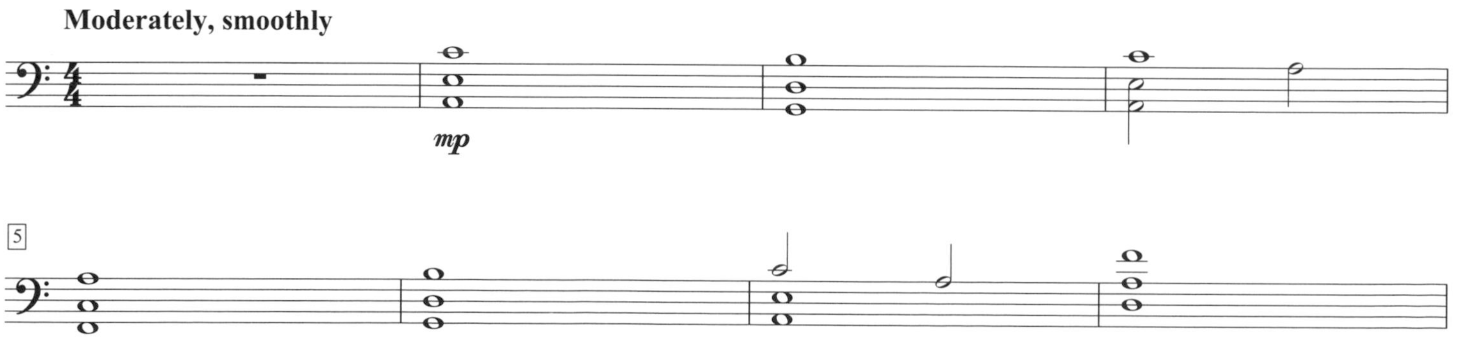
Moderately, smoothly
mp
5

© 2018 by The Willis Music Co.
International Copyright Secured All Rights Reserved

9
ex - ile here un - til the Son of God ap -

13
5
pear. Re - joice, re - joice! Em - man - u -
mf

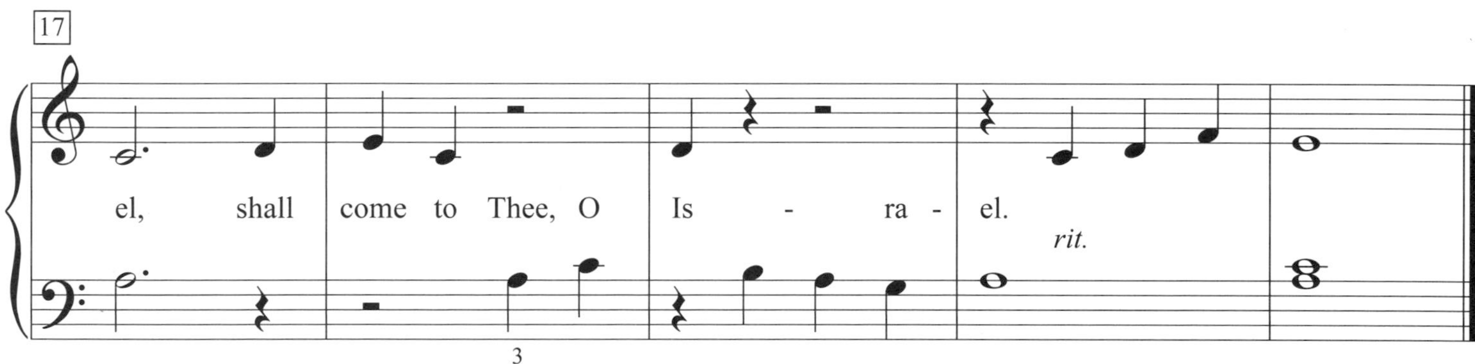
17
el, shall come to Thee, O Is - ra - el.
rit.
3

9
13
mf
17
rit.

Glenda Austin is a composer, arranger, pianist, and teacher who writes piano music popular at all levels. She graduated from the University of Missouri (Columbia) with a bachelor's degree in music education and a master's degree in piano performance. Glenda has over 40 years' experience as an elementary and high school music teacher, and holds memberships in the Music Teachers National Association and Missouri Music Educators Association. A frequent adjudicator and clinician, she has presented workshops for teachers and students throughout the United States, as well as in Canada and Japan. In addition, she is adjunct faculty and pianist for the chorale and vocal department at Missouri Southern State University. Married to high-school sweetheart, David, they are the parents of Susan and Scott, and grandparents of Isaac, Eden, and Levi.